To Ve
with
and many hap'i
Evan

The Triumph of Love

Evan John Jones

Howard Jones 02/14

CP

Cestrian Press

First Published in 2014 by:
Cestrian Press
13,Stanton Road,
Bebington,
Wirral.
CH63 3HN

A CIP Catalogue Record is available from The British Library

First Published 2014.
ISBN 978 0 904448 42 9

Printed and bound in Great Britain by:
Book Printing UK,
Remus House,
Coltsfoot drive,
Peterborough,
PE2 9JX

Contents

I dedicate these poems in memory of my dear late wife, Dilys. They are also for my lovely children and grandchildren, for family and friends, and for those who touched my life, sometimes passing 'like ships in the night', but enriching it, and contributing to the 'triumph of love'.

I especially dedicate this Collection to my very good friend of many years, Margaret Gillies Brown, Makar (Laureate) to 'Scottish Poetry', one of Scotland's leading poetry productions and author of numerous collections of published poems and prose works. I thank her with all my heart for her valuable suggestions, and for spending hours editing the poems. She also chose the title.

I would finally like to thank Kemal Houghton of The Chester Poets for his unstinting help in bringing this volume to fruition, and for publishing the final work.

Evan J Jones   December 2013.

Evan was born on the edge of the Llŷn Peninsula, North Wales, in 1934. He attended Pwllheli Grammar School and Bangor University, and subsequently taught at Holyhead, Bridgnorth and Gwynedd Technical College, Bangor. He married Dilys Roach in December 1962, and four children were born – David, Daniel, Arwel and Catherine. He spent most of his working life on Anglesey, moving to Llandudno after Dilys' death in 2005, and then to Northwich, Cheshire, in 2011. He is a past member of Elgin Writers, and a present member of Llandudno Writers and Chester Poets. He is the author of a children's book, published in Welsh and various poems and articles that have appeared in magazines and anthologies.

Foreword by Margaret Gillies Brown

'The Triumph of Love' is a good title for this delightful and well written collection. In one way or another love runs through these poems. First and foremost it is the love for his late wife in poems written with deep feeling and that yet manage to make the personal universal. For the rest his love and enthusiasm for life (a long one in his case - almost eighty years) shines through.

His subject matter is varied and his take on things sometimes unexpected and unique as in the 'Cull of the Gods' which explores a fairly recent event when a mountain in Iceland (Eyjafjallajokull), erupted. The poems, however, cover a wide time span progressing from his early memories of being brought up on a Welsh hillside in 'Childhood Home' 'Why do I love you?/you are nothing but a scrape of land/ on a lonely hill.,' to wartime memories of childhood in 'Evacuees' and 'Wartime games.' The latter can`t fail to bring tears to the eyes.

Most of all what I love about Evan's poetry is the feeling that runs through it which I often find lacking in many modern poems.

Some of the poems are humorous as in 'Miss Muffet and the Spider' , some tender as in his poem about a cat called Twgi, and some truly lyrical as in Kingsmead. Occasionally there are hints of a Celtic melancholy. There are one or two poems in Welsh, Evan`s native language which, he tells me, he spoke exclusively until he went to school. There is everything in this collection. Enjoy it.

ONE JULY SUNDAY IN LLANDUDNO
(24.07.11) by Margaret Gillies Brown

For Evan Jones

A water-colour blue
wide-sweep laps the shore.
All night, in the Summer dark,
gulls squabble around roof tops.
Now, sun dazzles the high Dover – white hotels
circling, admiring the bay.
You meet us in the doorway
with your Dylan Thomas voice, warm smile,
enthusiastic welcome...
People smile around you.
You whisk us off to a lavender village
where houses huddle in friendship:
treat us to a gourmet meal
in a wood-warm tavern.

Afterwards – the Great Orme:
monstrous cliff where white goats from Kashmir,
introduced a century ago,
climb rocky ledges with amazing skill.
From the green top –
a spectacular view.

To the south the legendary mountains:
to the north the endless ocean
where, in the distance,
pale ghosts with flailing arms
turn wind to usable energy.
With a poet's vision you see
the far horizon.
Joy turns to melancholy.
You ask, 'What lies beyond?'

CHILDHOOD HOME

Why do I love you?
You are nothing but a scrape of land
on a lonely hill.
Grey rocks scarring the barren fields,
and overgrown hedges, like tufts of wool
hanging on rusted barbed wire.
Snowdon silhouetted above you,
towering against the blue-black sky,
and summer storms sweeping from the west.

But why do I love you?
I have no climber's eye for Tryfan's grandeur,
nor his desire to challenge nature
by bouncing spider-like on trusty ropes.
I do not crave the tourist's
wish for solitude,
nor do I share his wonder at the
majesty of mountains.

It is a bitter beauty I see.
... I trudged these hills in childhood,
in sun and rain and wind ...
and later toiled, and tilled the sour soil,
'til freedom came
with my father's death ...
and then I left to follow dreams
in distant lands ...

And yet I love you still,
you scrape of land on a lonely hill.
But I know not why ... precisely.

EVACUEES

They fly in like swallows,
resting in the rafters
of our quiet Welsh homes,
away from the bombs.
Two of them, girls, perch on our spare bed
in the little farmhouse on the edge of the village.
Dad, who speaks little English, is at a loss.
Mam, who is kind, welcomes them with love.
I, being a boy, resent their coming,
and ignore them.
We, the lads, don't understand
their nasal Scouse, their strange ways.
We fight them in the fields, ignoring our elders,
who preach peace in dire times,
urging us to love our brothers... and sisters.

Then, in no time, they learn to speak Welsh,
our English improves, they teach us to swear –
dreadful dirty words. We love it!
Together we hide in hedgerows,
shooting down German 'planes.
They talk about Scottie Road and the Dingle,
and we laugh and climb trees,
making fun of Hitler.
We march behind the Home Guard,
go up the mountain looking out for the Invasion,
sandwiches in our gas-mask boxes,
and buttermilk to drink.
They help on the farm, gathering in the hay and corn;
they come to chapel to give thanks for the harvest.

We forget they are evacuees,
no different from us.

One day they fly away;
we don't feel much like playing.
Mam cries a little.

WAR RATIONS

'Sweet coupons, my lovely?'
Mrs Jones leans on her counter,
big bosom spread before me,
the squint in one eye the only blemish
in her old, beautiful face.
'All gone, Mrs Jones... sorry...'
'Never mind, *bach,* see what we can do.'
Gives me two gobstoppers from a jar,
leans closer and whispers, glancing round the empty shop,
'Not a word to anybody mind – *careless words cost lives.'*
'She'd be a great spy', I think to myself,
'but don't know how they'd drop her behind enemy lines.'

I go home for dinner, face severely swollen
by the gobstopper.
Dad is sitting at the table in front of a big plate of
new potatoes, newly dug,
two fresh eggs laid by our hens,
ham from our recently killed pig,
big lump of butter made by Mam,
and thick bread baked yesterday.
'Spit out that sweet,' says Mam,
putting a loaded plate in my place,
and she sits to join us while we eat in silence.

'Rations!' says Dad, drinking his tea
sitting in his armchair, after stirring in two spoonsful of sugar,
'Don't know how we manage indeed...
time this old war came to an end...'

WARTIME GAMES

Rrrrrr... rrrrrr... Wheeee... rrrrrr!   I'm a Spit!
Rat... rattattat.... Ack... ackackack!   Got you Messerschmitt!
Wowwowwow... Whaaaaw!   I've done my bit!

Bang... bang... bang!   My wooden gun's hot!
Lie down, Johnny Long... I know I got
you in the 'ead!   Alive you're not!

Pow-wow... pow-pow!   Grenades fall!
Whoooosh... whoosh!   Smashed you all!
After you're dead we'll then play ball...

Charge with bayonets over the hill!
Scream aloud, 'Kill! Kill! Kill!'
Chase the Hun! Shoot at will...

On Sunday morn the sun shines bright,
Inside the Church all peace and light.
The preacher says, 'You must not kill;
pray for peace and be quite still;
love your foe, dispense with hate...
That's the way to the Golden Gate.'

Rattattat... rattat... tattat... we fly from Church;
guns all blazing at a bird on a perch.
We shout together, 'Hate! Hate! Hate!'
And forget all about the Golden Gate.

But Johnny Long, whose dad is dead,
walks slowly home, his eyes all red.

LOSERS

I played in goal in nineteen-forty-six,
between two coats laid down upon the beach.
They had eleven, but we were in a fix,
with only nine, a full team out of reach.
Titch Morgan had to play, or was it mime?
Knew nothing about football, not a clue –
he played for us from kick-off to half-time,
then played for them until the whistle blew.
I watched Titch Morgan growing to a man;
was saddened by his knack to self-destruct -
still playing for the other side, and ran
in circles, and was very often sucked
into a life of crime, and in a fix.
We lost that match in nineteen-forty-six.

WHY?

Dad! Dad! Why is the sky blue?
Why is grass green, and what is glue?
Why do horses neigh, and dogs bark?
Where does the sun go when it's dark?
'I don't know, do I?'

Dad! Dad! Why is lemon sour?
Why are there petals on a flower?
Why are trees so thick and tall?
And why, in autumn, do leaves fall?
'I don't know, do I?'

Dad! Dad! Why is jam so sticky?
Why do they call a little mouse Mickey?
Why doesn't an aeroplane fall from the sky?
Why do sweets cost so much to buy?
'I don't know, do I?'

Dad! Dad! why is my sister so spotty,
and taking so long to use a potty?
Why do you scratch your chin with your finger?
Why does Mum make us all eat ginger?
'I don't know, do I?'

Dad! Dad! I hope you don't really mind
me asking these questions, 'cause you are so kind.
'Not at all, Johnny, what I always say
is that's how children learn, at the end of the day.'

ESCAPE INTO CELLULOID

A wet Saturday night in Pwllheli.
We, the lads, long ago in our Youth,
in the warmth of the Palladium
waiting for a feast of films.
Lights full on, screen curtained, music playing;
and a special cinema smell mingling with the aroma
of wet clothes drying.
Watching the local girls coming in –
young hopefuls in powder and paint,
dolled-up and exciting...
that is until the lights dim and the film starts,
and then WOW!
Beautiful goddesses with long limbs and glistening lips,
peeping white flesh and inviting eyes
entice us into a sunlit land full of heroes,
and inept villains;
cowboys in clean Stetsons and dust-free chaps,
six guns low in holsters, eyes squinting,
and lightning fast on the draw.
The handsome one always gets the girl,
by treating her meanly, mainly,
but in the end walking with her hand-in-hand,
past the cactus, into the distant sunset...

And we, the lads, not waiting for the Anthem,
rush to catch the last bus home, but with enough time
to roll and swagger from side to side,
hands low over imaginary holsters,
and mean eyes looking from left to right;
some of us hurling a punch or two
at dancing shadows in the dark...

18

'Come on, you lot,' shouts the conductor,
'or you won't get home 'til morning...'

WHO KNOWS?

When my father married my mother
he was forty. She was older.
Good match, or a desperate attempt
to Live?
They doted on me, of course,
and they spoilt me rotten
- well, my mother did.

Were they to know then
that dreams are false?
That poverty destroys?
That sulky silence kills love?
And that nothing lasts?

Had he remained a bachelor –
blue serge suit, gold tooth, and fine brown boots –
would he have been happier?
Had she remained a spinster -
hard working but carefree –
would she have found peace?

Who knows?
And if that were the case
I wouldn't be here
to ask these questions.
Would I?

MISS MUFFET AND THE SPIDER

Little Miss Muffet sat down for her dinner
and shouted quite loudly at her hard-working mother,
'Mummy, what is there to eat today?'
'Why, dear, as always it's curds and whey.'
Miss Muffet got into the most fearful mood –
she was always quite fussy about her food;
'But Mummy, I want something better than that –
some bacon or sausages sizzling in fat.'
'But you know, my dear, that we haven't got any...
we're far too poor - we haven't a penny
to spend on food that the rich people eat...
I'm sorry, my dear, but we can't afford meat.'

Miss Muffet stormed out with her curds and whey
and sat on her tuffet for the rest of the day;
she just couldn't face that tasteless fare,
and sobbed and cried, 'it's not fair, not fair!'
High up above her on a branch of a tree
a spider sat looking, and thought he could see
some delicate titbits that would do for a meal,
so he quickly descended on his silken reel.
He landed in the middle of Miss Muffet's plate
and started eating at quite an astonishing rate.
Miss Muffet saw him and gobbled him whole,
smacked her lips and said, 'Well, bless my soul,
that's the nicest meal I have ever eaten,'
and she sighed with pleasure and purred like a kitten.

When she went inside she said to her mother,
'I've just eaten a spider and would lo-ove another.'

WHAT IS IT ALL ABOUT?

What's all this talk
of tsunamies and storms?
Floods and ferocious winds,
twisters and tumbleweed,
drought and disasters?
What's it all about –
this talk of global warming,
damaged ozone layer
and melting Pole caps?
What's it all about?

'Lovely day!' we used to say.
'Looks like rain doesn't it?'
'Frost tonight?'
How predictably unpredictable
was the weather – then!
But now it has become
predictably threatening!
No longer the soft soaking
of a springtime shower.
No longer the hazy heat
of sun-dried cornfields.
No longer frost-filled streams
and lonely blizzard-bound farms.
No longer the silly British Weather –
predictably unpredictable!
What's it all about?

Seasons have merged.
Plants flower twice –
conned into believing that it's spring again!
Tropical storms hit Tewkesbury,
and it's hell in Hull!
Monsoons engulf the Midlands,
and Rotherham is rain-drenched!
Boscastle is bogged down,
and Carlisle is in chaos!
What's it all about?

We seek an answer.
We dangle twixt doom and disbelief.

What is it all about?

WEATHER OR NOT

I'm reducing my carbon footprint
to try and save the world,
to bring back again the weather
we had in days of old.

To savour the magic springtime
with breezes and sunshine and rain,
those balmy days of summer,
that golden autumn again.

To wake of a winter's morning
with a sprinkling of snow on the byre;
to ramble the icy hillside,
then sit by a blazing fire.

To see the snowdrops in season
and 'daffs' on Saint David's Day,
to welcome the April showers
and the beautiful flowers of May.

To think of the little hedgehog
sleeping for months in the dark,
and squirrels resting in hollows,
snugly behind the bark...

I'm reducing my carbon footprint
by walking everywhere,
I limit my breathing and sweating
just in case I pollute the air!

I sit wrapped up in my bedroom
suffering the darkness and cold.
The food I eat is organic,
and I'm hoping to grow quite old.

But will it be worth it I wonder –
what if it's all in vain?
What hope, with global warming,
of restoring the balance again?

CULL OF THE GODS

Eyjafjallajokull!
You spewed the contents of your burning belly,
red-hot lava and blue-black smoke,
so high into the sky
that clouds of prickly ash
came drifting
southwards –
covering the earth
and causing chaos
everywhere!
You did what the Luftwaffe failed to do,
and grounded planes
in Britain's green and pleasant land!
And you, Mighty Man,
Master of the Universe,
Creator of all things
too wonderful to know –
Yes you!
You were left cringing as you have so often been,
threatened by floods and pestilence,
by fire and awesome storms,
impotent in the face of this Icelandic ash
and unable to control the forces
that bear upon your little life!
You thought that you could harness
wind and wave, and tame the oceans,
but Nature promises there is more to come
to undermine your hopes!
The gods continue with their cull!
O mighty, angry, awe-ful Eyjafjallajokull.

TWGI

Small black-and-white bundle
of energy and charm –
a treasure called Twgi.
A kitten all her life,
full of fun,
mischievous as a street urchin;
one minute sleeping on your lap,
the next swinging trapeze-like
from a curtain;
sliding stealthily into next-door's kitchen
to pinch a pork chop
defrosting on the sink-top;
visiting neighbours
to be fed and fussed over,
but never growing fat.
She was an elegant pursuer
of mouse and bird,
proud to bring back prey,
and leave it dead and bloody on the doorstep.
Chose a bird table for afternoon nap -
surprised when the birds
preferred to starve.
A cat that never took umbrage,
bouncing back from any telling-off,
as full of love as ever.

She lived with us for years,
then one cold morning
I took Twgi to the vet.
Returned home - alone.

LAZING ON A SUNDAY AFTERNOON

I sit by the sleeping stream,
distant bells calling me to church;
insects hovering above the still water,
seemingly unaware that,
below the surface,
predators are poised for their leap,
seeking to destroy.
I am oblivious to it all,
lulled into a stupor
by the warm sun
and heady fragrance
of Nature's myriad plants.
I listen for wind in the trees
and Mister Toad's croaking.
No sound.
I savour the silence,
as I seek solitude
and perfect peace...

Whirrrang... Whirrang... Whirrang!

I sit up.
Birds break from the branches
and flee into the blue.
Small animals scuttle in the slime,
and fish keep their heads
under water.

It must be a chain-saw!
Man on a mission to destroy.

I linger awhile.
Should I stay
to recapture the silence?
Or has it gone for ever –
shattered by someone
with a different agenda
from mine?

REASON TO LIVE
(In memory of Michael Todd, former Chief Constable of Greater Manchester Police)

What were your thoughts
as the snow and ice of Snowdon
closed around you?
Did you feel regret or fear or sadness
as you swigged the spirits,
and sensed the chill creeping
into your bones?
Did you think of family,
friends, lovers, colleagues,
as you were about to die
alone in Eryri?
Was there not one reason,
one tiny reason,
to live?
To seek the sun?
To make amends?
To ask forgiveness?
To try and face the burden
that drove you
to this barren land
with night closing in
around you?
Just one tiny,
tiny reason
to live?

MIDSUMMER

It was midsummer when Drake
finished his game of bowls
before dispatching the Armada.

It was midsummer when `planes
filled blue skies over England,
spitting fire and defeating the Foe.

It was midsummer when the ships
crossed the Channel on D-Day,
carrying troops to march on Europe.

It was midsummer when riots
broke out in Alabama,
in order to realise a Dream.

Tell me, is Man at his worst
when Nature is at her best?
Or is it just an illusion?

THE SIEGE OF TROY

The Trojans looked out one bright morning,
saw millions of ships out at sea;
someone shouted, 'the Greekos are coming!
They want us to bend at the knee.'

'Can't say I'm surprised,' muttered Hector
to his brother, so wayward and weak.
'Should have left that Helen alone, boy.
Now see what you've done, silly geek!'

No time to give too many details
of the Siege of that City called Troy –
lasted yonks after Hector was slaughtered
by Achilles, not one of the low hoi-polloi.

But the siege was broken one morning
by a large wooden horse seen on beach;
Trojans thought `twas a gift from the Greekos
and brought it inside out of reach

of thieves and other no-gooders
 – thought the Greekos had all gone away –
but that night out jumped all the soldiers,
and Achaea at last won the day.

Nowadays, we can all enjoy watching
the film with the pretty Brad Pitt –
makes everything look so exciting,
not at all like it was, not a bit.

GLIMPSE INTO THE PAST

In this place yesterday creeps in
and pushes today out of the way:
the azure sky turns black,
the trees of summer become skeletal,
the warm breeze turns into a chill wind;
today becomes yesterday.

Out of the ruins the castle grows again, and lives –
the cry of the archer is heard on the ramparts,
the bustle of life inside the walls
as they try to withstand the siege.
Rocks are hurled from towers,
boiling liquid poured on attackers,
flimsy ladders pushed back,
swords thrust as heads appear,
and blood is spilt.
When a lull comes bodies are rested,
the wounded tended and sleep snatched.
Another attack. Cries of despair,
'The Prince is dead!'
The drawbridge drops and in they come,
looting and raping and killing...

The noise abates, the sky lightens,
the trees are green again in the warm breeze,
moss covers the fallen walls,
and today returns.

SOLDIERS

We fought on the fringes of Jerusalem with Richard,
charged with Harry at Agincourt,
slaughtered at Culloden, bled at Waterloo,
endured the cold of Crimea and the Indian heat;
slithered in the Flanders mud and sweated at Tobruk.
We shook with fear on the hills of Korea,
and in the jungles of Vietnam.
We yomped across the Falklands,
despaired at Bosnia and the Gulf,
braved Iraq and Afghanistan and asked,
'what next and why?'
Was it for King and Country?
For God and Justice?
For Freedom and a Better World?
Or was it for ideals plucked out of the air
by politicians safe on their plush green seats,
ruled by greed and power?
Who knows.

We are the dead –
hollow holes in skulls beneath the soil of distant lands;
bones scattered over vast continents;
blood dried and mingled with the now green earth
under stark white crosses.
Songs are sung;
poems written;
memorials built;
graves attended and words muttered,
'No more! No more!'
and pretending that we *grow not old*.
But avoiding the eternal WHY?

LASSIE WITH THE LAMP

Through broken windows
of the broken barrack hospital at Scutari
the moon shone on Billy Briggs.
'Pale lassie of the lamp', he thought,
propping himself on pulverised pillow,
bandaged head throbbing,
mouth dry as the summer hay
he used to mow so long ago.

'Nurse!'
It was her lamp he saw first,
light permeating the dark;
and then *she* came.
'All right, Billy...'
She wet his lips with water
that tasted like wine;
she touched his brow
with soft, cool fingers;
she unpulverised his pillow;
she spoke words of hope.
'Ta, Miss Nightingale...
my lassie with the lamp...'
he murmured on the edge of sleep.

By dawn Billy Briggs was dead.
When they took him away
she sighed with sadness,
resolving to do more
for every broken Billy
at Scutari

SCARS OF BATTLE

'Not a scratch on 'im... lucky bugger!'
His mates at the pub welcomed him back
from The Great War.
'So glad you're home safely, love,'
whispered his doting wife,
caressing his white, unblemished body;
and his children were proud of their hero-father.

'Must have been hell over there?'
some queried, but he said not a word.
'Was it as bad as they say?'
questioned others, but his lips were tight.
He went about his work on the farm as before,
but woke up screaming in the night.
He was morose most of the time,
quick with his fists at the slightest quip;
walked the hills in the dark, muttering to himself.
His mates kept away;
his wife became fearful of his moods,
and his children cowered in corners
when he was around.
'Is he off his rocker?' they asked;
'not a scratch on 'im, lucky bugger...
probably *played possum* in No Man's Land!'
'Leave 'im alone, I says, if that's what 'e wants.'
He failed to turn up at the farm for days...
'AWOL,' laughed someone,
who had never been *over there.*

He disappeared for weeks
and returned the worse for wear;
became violent to his family
and cried with remorse.
'Lucky bugger,' they said,
'could 'ave been blinded, or gassed;
or lost a leg... or an arm... or both!'

They found him hanging in the barn
one winter's day.
They followed the coffin up the hill, dressed in black,
and some wept in the wind and rain;
and the vicar spoke vaguely
of the 'scars of battle and the waste of war.'

OVER THERE
(to the dead of World War 1)

They left farms and factories,
families and friends, fields and forests,
and sailed over there.

They marched through mud and marshes,
through madness and mayhem,
somewhere over there.

They fought the foe in trenches,
endured endless days of horror,
and hell over there.

They died dreadful deaths,
lie buried 'neath neat white crosses,
still over there.

SURVIVAL

I hovered above the clouds,
eyes peeled for Messerschmitts,
heart in mouth but elated
at the thought of battle.
Suddenly, from above, they appeared.
I sent the Spit into a dive
before climbing steeply, guns blazing,
pursuing them through the wide and endless sky.
I remember little about it
except the trails of smoke and the noise,
the falling metal and whine of engines,
and the leaping flames...
and the sun shining
on silver clouds.

Back at base they said,
'Well done!'
I gave thanks.
I had survived.

HOLOCAUST

It was the pile of spectacles
that stood out
in that hell
called Dachau...
Twisted bits of wire
begging the question
of who wore them?
As their owners lined up naked,
waiting for the gas-chambers,
what were their thoughts?
Did they recall happier times
with family and friends,
plying their trade and
picnicking on sunny afternoons?
Or were they numb, dehumanised
by the inhumanity of those
who removed
their spectacles?

LONELY NEW YEAR

Big Ben exploded into shafts of light
as revellers to the old year waved goodbye.
She sat alone and watched the merry sight
on a screen so very small it hurt the eye.

When morning chased away the fading moon
she still sat huddled in her lonely chair,
the screen still flickered darkly in the room,
no friendly footstep sounded on the stair.

THIRD-MILLENNIUM CHRISTMAS

It's christmas again,
with carols sung half-heartedly
in empty churches.
The faithful come
tearful and redundant;
the silent night is shattered
by the raucous ranting of the rabble.
The old myths are barely remembered.
And the magic has gone.

It's Midwinter again –
no longer bleak and ice-bound;
no longer dark and grim
in a global-warmed world.
The neon lights obliterate the stars,
and ringing tills announce the profits
of the monolithic stores.
And saturnalia-like the populace is caught
in an orgy of merrymaking,
while lonely druids celebrate
the Solstice.

And in this bleak christmastide
man is torn between belief
and non-belief.
No longer able to wonder at a baby
born in a stable;
no longer able to join the shepherds
on an angel-lit hill,
or follow the magi star.

No longer able to rise above
the mundane,
the ordinary,
the every-day,
the cheap,
the now,
and only now.

But longing too
for Hope and Good News,
for Good-will and Love,
and Peace on Earth.

Longing perhaps for Christmas.

SIDNEY SMART

This is the tale of Sidney Smart
who hated Christmas with all his heart;
so every year, come early December
he'd get all het-up with a face like thunder.

He hated the lights and the sparkling trees,
and the mention of turkeys and fat white geese.
He hated the shops with their ringing tills
(though he himself didn't have any bills!)

He hated the sight of the Santa Clauses
with their long curly beards and bright red noses.
He hated the singing of 'Silent Night',
and the tinsel and trimmings so shining bright.

He hated the names Rudolph, Noel and Chris,
and to hear 'Christina' put him in a right tiz!
But above all he hated the Christmas Fairy,
and the old, old story of Joseph and Mary.

So Sid spent December in deep, deep gloom,
shut up for hours in his dark little room;
waiting for another new year to dawn
and a chance, once again, for a different moan!

But for those who enjoy a happy ending,
just wait a mo' – there's one just pending!

For one fine morning in early May
a girl called Carol came Sidney's way –
they fell deeply in love, and our Sid found a reason
to know the true meaning of the Festive Season.

THE MAGI STAR SPEAKS
(In memory of Sir Patrick Moore, CBE, 1923 - 2012)

Patrick Moore,
had you been there long ago,
I'm sure you would have seen me
through your monocle.
You could have been one of the Magi,
talking quickly and showing the way.
You'd have argued that it was not I who was moving,
but rather Planet Earth on its axis...
Bethlehem travelling towards me,
and not the other way round.
You'd have made that long journey shorter
by your wit and knowledge,
and would have convinced the ages to come
that it was all true,
that strange happening in a cradle
in the City of David...
that it wasn't just a story to fit a prophecy,
Church theology to persuade its people,
a myth to please children,
something convenient for creators of carols,
a selling point for superstores,
a feel-good factor for folk at Christmastime.

Thank you, Patrick, for a lifetime of telling
that mysteries still remain
in the sky at night.

LONELINESS

'I wander'd lonely as a cloud'
wrote Wordsworth when in pensive mood;
I wonder why he'd chosen 'cloud'
to paint a state of solitude -
why not as lonely as a tramp
walking the roads all cold and damp?

Why not a pilgrim or a straying dog,
a Nomad or a Romany?
A weary traveller lost in fog,
a sailor in a storm at sea?
I think of this when oft I lie
upon my couch, with inward eye.

Why not indeed? I ponder long
on many poems that Wordsworth wrote -
a reaper girl could do no wrong,
on Lucy Gray he seemed to dote.
In loneliness he seems to find
something outside the human mind,

something that's written in our fate,
something within our very souls,
something beyond this earthly state,
something expressed in pains and woes...
Like clouds that come and wander by,
silent and lonely in the sky.

DAWN

The silence of the night is broken.
A faint light permeates the dark
as dawn breaks on a far horizon.
A bird's cry, hesitant, is heard.
The stars pale
and the moon wanes
as the Earth moves and slowly wakes
from hours of slumber.
Wonder of wonders,
another day is born.

And you, man of the third millennium,
afraid of the uncertain darkness of our times,
afraid of slipping back into eternal chaos,
afraid lest culture die and love should perish...
You, creature of this age,
must think again;
and in your weakness listen for the birdsong.
You must believe that light
will bring again a glorious dawn.

LOST LOVE

I'm leaving this on your pillow
- the conch we brought back with us
from that distant island long ago.
And when you gently wake perhaps
the swishing sound of rippling waves
will steal upon you in your slumber,
and bring back love into your soul.
We were young – then.
We had hopes and visions
as we lay upon that golden beach...
our fingers touched amid the sand and pebbles,
and time stopped...

We dreamt so often to return upon the tide,
to that distant island far away;
to capture what we felt, so long ago...
but dreams die in humdrum days
of unchanging reality,
and love is lost...

I leave this conch at your ear
in the small still hours before the dawn;
and as I steal away upon the tide
I hope, some day, to find our island,
and that you will again
return to me.

ALL A DREAM?

Do you remember that midsummer night
in the long ago?
Do you recall the soft rustle of leaves
in the trees,
and the aroma of pine?
Do you still see the light of the moon
peeping between the branches,
and hear the patter of tiny beings
in the undergrowth of the forest floor?
And the flutter of our hearts?
Do you remember how I touched your face,
and tasted your lips,
and said that I loved you?
How I called you *Hermia* to my *Lysander*,
and how I told you
that I needed no love potion
to open my eyes
to your beauty and your wonder?

And now, that you are with me no more,
do you, too, think
that it might all
have been a dream?

THE PRICE OF LOVE

When I was young and foolish
I thought that love was free
like flowers in the hedgerow
and leaves upon a tree –
no price on love for me.

But now that I am older
I count the cost of love
in pain and sacrifices -
the hawk has killed the dove.
That is the price of love.

MYFANWY

Schubert sought his Sylvia,
and Galway's Annie fluted
some long-lost yearning.
Corelli mandolined his Pelagia,
and Lara's sadness themed the
white vastness that was Zhivago.
But Parry's Myfanwy... Ah!
The greatest love song of them all,
at any time, in any place,
in any language.
The Welsh Myfanwy exudes *hiraeth,*
that untranslatable word
beyond longing.
But it's not about her, but him –
the rejected lover pouring out
his heartache in words and music,
echoing the loss of ten thousand sweethearts
throughout the ages.
The ire of her dark eyes
contrasts with her gentleness,
and his undying love forgives Myfanwy,
wishing her a lifetime bathed in mid-day sunshine,
and the red red rose of well-being for ever
dancing on her cheeks.
And like the wounded Robbie
he asks only
for a last farewell.

A DIFFICULT CHOICE

Old Thomas had always been fond of his beer,
and when he was drunk he tended to leer
at any young girl who passed him by –
his florid face flushed and a glint in his eye.

His wife, Mary Jane, didn't like this a bit –
she would rant and rave, and would fall in a fit;
she would drag Old Tom home and give him hell,
kick his ankles and push him, and clout him as well.

Her husband would finally fall back on the bed,
pretending to be, to all appearances, dead.
His dear wife then would quietly weep,
and give him a cuddle 'til he fell asleep.

But one day she gave him an ultimatum,
and said, 'You must choose between me and Satan!'
Old Tom, cold sober now and feeling much pain,
said, 'I'll miss you so much, my sweet Mary Jane.'

ISLANDS

'No one is an island,'
said the Poet;
'no one lives for himself,
by himself,
like a pelican in the wilderness.
Everyone is part of the whole;
everyone, in some way, is tied
to someone, somewhere, sometime,
and each death is a loss.'

'Everyone is an island,'
said the Iron Lady;
'it's everyone for himself,
ploughing his own furrow,
living his own life,
independent of family,
and community,
and nation...
on your bike, mate!
If you can't survive...
Tough!'

Perhaps the truth is
somewhere in between...
Each island has its two poles.
Each island is dependent on others –
the small boat that braves the foaming sea;
sound waves that bring voices
to fill the void;
the `copter that carries aid in distress
- lifelines to loneliness.

But each island, too, is inward
in its thinking;
narrow in its vision
with little beyond the horizon;
and inbreeding mummifying the mind.

We, too, islanders of a kind,
are torn between two poles.
Longing for companionship and love;
for warmth and comfort from the storms of life;
for someone to care...
and yet, we crave freedom;
to release the hand that guides us;
to let go of the apron strings
and cross the threshold
in search of Nirvana,
and the Avalon of dreams.

IN YNYS MÔN – *IN THE ISLE OF ANGLESEY*

In Ynys Môn the air is pure,
which makes the place to me so dear;
around its shores the sea shines bright
and sparkles under stars at night,
and walking there I feel no fear.

'Twas when I left I shed a tear,
but in my heart it's always near.
I've often longed to see the light
in Ynys Môn.

I wonder if again I'll hear
the water lapping in the mere;
I wonder if one day I might
return once more and set my sight
on seas so blue and skies so clear
in Ynys Môn.

KINGSMEAD

Have you ever been to Kingsmead
when Spring is in the air?
Have you ever spent an evening
in the woods, without a care?
Have you lingered by the Weaver,
watching the anglers wait,
patiently by the long poles,
for fish to nibble the bait?

Have you ever seen the white swans
swimming silently by?
Have you listened in the twilight
to hear the heron's cry?
Have you ever seen the ducklings
flapping wings in case they sank?
Have you noticed how the barges
snuggle against the bank?

I've never been to The Gambia,
I've never been to Bhutan,
I've never crossed The Andes,
I've never been to Japan;
but I know that if I travel
to countries far and fair,
there's nowhere quite like Kingsmead
when Spring is in the air.

(Kingsmead is a wooded area by the River Weaver on the outskirts of Northwich in Cheshire.)

FROM THE TOP OF A DOUBLE DECKER BUS

High above ground I have the top deck to myself.
I intend to read my book,
but seeing beyond the hedgerows, walls and fences,
I am captivated by the vista of this,
as yet unseen, new world.
I see money oozing out of large clipped lawns,
and manorial Cheshire houses;
I see chalets and luxurious sheds,
flower beds and fountains, pergolas and pools,
and near-naked bodies sizzling in the summer sun.
I look down on expensive cars,
on a World of Wealth.

My book remains unopened.
I take in the rural landscape –
tiny farmers on toy tractors,
bales of hay beyond a five-barred gate,
yellowing corn, cattle lying in the heat,
sheep curled up like white candy floss,
and lonely cottages tucked into green glades.
I pass allotments and greenhouses,
I see flora on forest floors,
and fields fading into the distant horizon.
Looking ahead I see the outline of the City,
dozing in the shimmering haze;
and getting closer, buildings and churches,
and a glimpse of the river,
winding towards the centre;
barges tied up by the banks,
little craft gliding under bridges,
and people walking by the water.

Soon it'll be journey's end,
and the private world I've seen
will be but a memory, with one or two regrets...
with the rumbling of the bus it was a silent world,
no birdsong or the voices of people to be heard
or the sound of silence;
a sterile world, without the smell of summer,
of pine and peonies;
a distant world where nature was seen,
but not felt.

BONJOUR

I sit at the little round table,
metallic and gaily painted;
finish my *croque monsieur,*
and sip my *Beaujolais.*
'Plaisir d'amour' fills the fragrant air,
as trim waitresses, in black slit-skirts
and little round caps,
float around the sunlit café,
with *L'arc De Triomphe* and *La Tour Eiffel*
decorating the walls.

Phillipe approaches...
'Bonjour – is all *très bon?'*
'Oui, Phillipe. Merci – thank you.'
'Would *Monsieur* like a *crêpe?'*
'Non – no thank you, Phillipe.'
'Bon,' and he drifts away.
I finish my wine.
I lean back and close my eyes...

'Everything OK, luv?'
asks the waitress
as she clears the table.
'Yes, fine,' I say, and slip out
into the wet Rochdale street.

DAY'S END

There is something sad about Mostyn Street
at a quarter-past-five
every day.
Some shops closed early,
others smelling of disinfectant
as assistants anticipate
the ending of the day.
Goods dragged in off pavements;
tills totted up;
coats donned,
ready for the off.
Security barriers noisily pulled down,
leaving the street to loiterers
and litter.
Window displays droop
as night closes in –
no one to entice.
Darkness will soon fall
bringing fear of smashed glass
and raucous roarings
of revellers and vandals.
Decent folk hurry home,
leaving Mostyn Street
to nightfall and another day.

YESTERDAY

We stopped at the end of the drive.
I asked the Agency girl,
'Can I go in on my own?'
Surprised, she handed me the heavy key.
I walked alone up the weed-strewn path.
She thought it was a first-time viewing.

The paint, now peeling on the door,
is still the same deep blue,
but now blackened with age.
The key turns noisily, and the creaking sound
opens on the old familiar hallway.
A piece of ivy brushes my hair
as I walk into yesterday.
I look up at the broken plaster,
cobwebs on cornices,
bats fluttering above...
My heart breaks.
Is that music I can hear
through the morning-room door?
Is that the rustle of a skirt,
and the smell of something sweet?
A beam of light shines through the cobwebs,
and slowly, very slowly, life returns
and I am young again.
A babble of voices fills the air;
friendly arms reach out,
and welcome me home
to the house I had left
so long ago...

'Why so long?' the voices whisper,
'Why so long... so long?'

'You OK, sir?' asked the girl from the Agency,
'Thought you were a bit long.'

TODAY

Today is yesterday's tomorrow,
and tomorrow will soon be today;
but 'tis no use living in sorrow –
today is yesterday's tomorrow.
In life we are anxious to borrow
more time from day to day –
Today is yesterday's tomorrow,
and tomorrow will soon be today.

OLD AGE

Growing older, I am told,
is much preferred to growing old;
older's with you all your life –
days keep passing, birthdays rife.
Old, however, is a state
without a discount or rebate –
now you're cornered in one place,
without much view, without much space;
many think that you are daft...
when was the last time that you laughed?

I'm growing older by the hour,
but fight old age with all my power.

DECIDOPHOBIA *(fear of making decisions)*

It's all Hamlet's fault –
just couldn't make up his mind
whether or not to despatch his step-dad
to another world.
'To be or not to be,' he soliloquised
(procrastinating they call it),
and now everyone's doing it
to avoid making decisions...
... er... sorry... sorry, but I must break off here...
thought I was going to write about decidophobia...
but now I'm not sure... er...
perhaps I should have chosen another subject...
Sorry... but I'm always like this...
often thinking how I'd like to be an optimist
but never sure if I could make it.
Hate going to restaurants
and having to choose from the menu...
when my meal comes
I look around and wish
I'd chosen someone else's fare.
Could never decide what to call my children...
that's why all nine of them have nine names... each...
eighty-one in all, and I'm never very sure
what to call them... each one.
Have lived in umpteen houses
but never stayed long...
always left the *FOR SALE* sign up for a while,
just in case I'd made a mistake.
Don't know whether to write any more now,
or just leave it as it is... it's an awful thing...
this *decidophobia.*

GREETINGS STRANGER *(Message in a bottle)*

I greet you, stranger, in some distant land;
on sunny shores, or midst the snow and ice
of northern wastes. To you I give my hand
in friendship and in language free from lies.
It was a whim that made me want to write
to you, who hopefully can rise above
those who would judge me, be it wrong or right;
those who hate, and those blinded by their love.
And so, inside this bottle you will find,
together with this preface to it all,
a plea for help, or maybe just some kind
of purging of the soul, to set my stall.
Therefore, dear stranger, will you please read on,
and keep me in your thoughts when I am gone...

RIGHT OR WRONG?

'It's wrong to kill - Right?'
'Wrong - it's OK if you do it for us, your Government...
for Queen and Country, and to destroy the enemy.'
'But what about God?'
'We don't do God.'

'It's wrong to steal - Right?'
'Wrong – it's OK if you are clever...
Ho! Ho! Ho! like stealing pensions.'
'But my conscience wouldn't let me.'
'We don't do Conscience.'

'Must be wrong to lust after someone's wife - Right?
'Wrong - it's OK as long as you're not found out...
happens all the time in politics, and everywhere.'

'But I think it's all wrong!'
'We don't do Wrong – Right?'

'Wrong!'

BULLDOZER

He was a bulldozer of a man –
arms angled and extended,
lifting and digging
with enormous strength,
a valuable member of the road-building gang.
He rumbled into her life,
refusing to be halted;
pushed and shoved her into corners;
removed her from her family
as easily as a clod of earth,
and carried her to distant places
with a roar and a whine.
And in time he dug her grave.

HORSEWOMAN

She pranced into town, on the highest of heels,
clip-clopping her way to the nearest bar;
teeth protruding, nostrils flared,
shaking loose her long blond mane.
She wiggled her buttocks
at the staring stallions,
snorted when bothered,
whinnied when pleased,
refused to be bridled or haltered or reined.

DISTANT VOICES

I can hear distant voices...
children in the playground,
neighbours bickering,
swimmers on the beach,
crowds in the stadium,
television programmes penetrating
the wafer-thin walls of my flat...

I can hear other distant voices,
wafting over the years...
Dad scolding, Mam fussing,
friends and enemies
praising and mocking,
teachers urging,
family supporting,
colleagues cajoling;
and my dear dead wife
imploring me
to *Carpe Diem* it,
and upping and going it...

If I care to I can switch off
these distant voices,
but not for long.

ONCE AGAIN

We thought we had finished with all that –
that men were no longer
doomed to die
in the bowels
of the earth;
that Senghenydd and Gresford had been
consigned to history;
that danger had disappeared in this
health-and-safety-lily-livered-nanny-state;
that technology had advanced,
and that, in any case,
Coal was Dead.

We reckoned without
The Gleision Pit.
An autumn Thursday
darkened into winter,
when men were, once again,
trapped below in the flooded dark.
The Media came.
Three miners escaped.
Four remained – their fate unknown.

Rescue teams converged
from everywhere,
and we waited and waited,
and hoped for two long days...
But it was not to be.
No Chilean repeat.
No euphoric joy –
just four men dying in the dark.

And David Alexander
will still be singing *The Price of Coal.*

(On Thursday, 15 September 2011 the privately owned Gleision Colliery in the Swansea Valley became flooded, and four men died three hundred feet underground. For 30 hours rescue services tried to save them, but to no avail. David Alexander, a Welsh born singer, had a 'hit' called The Price of Coal, the real price being the lives of the men who dug for it.)

LAST EXIT

As the final curtain falls
I glimpse the empty stage,
the spotlight
fading
away.

I remove my make-up,
my features old in the mirror.
I hang up my costume
for the last time,
the script is closed,
the last prompt made,
props taken away,
stage hands gone home,
no fans waiting at the door.

I walk away preparing
for my final role –
Retired-Has-Been
trudging lonely streets,
draining glasses alone,
reliving Hamlets of the past
and Lears that moved audiences
into tears.
I can still hear the adulation of crowds,
feel the pressure of fans,
see flashing bulbs of photographers,
sense the eagerness of reporters
pursuing their latest story.
I can still smell the theatre,
and recall heights I once touched...

The curtain's down,
the spotlight faded...
but the Fat Lady is yet to sing...

EIRA GWANWYN

Heddiw, disgynaist yn gwrlid distaw, gwyn,
ar ddaear llawn gwanwyn.
Ataliwyd chwrli'r cerbydau;
arafwyd bywyd wrth i bobl fethu a chyrraedd gwaith.
'Roedd dy ddychan tawel yn yr aer
yn gwawdio'r gwybodusion am feddwl
fod gwanwyn mor gynnar.
Awgrymaist y posibilrwydd o burdeb...
y gallai'r hen fyd 'ma fod yn well lle,
efo'r trigolion yn fwy gonest a glan;
heb gymaint o ruthro a rhegi,
trachwant a thrais.
Fuo'r hen dir 'ma 'rioed mor wyn o'r blaen
- gwynach na gwyn –
a'r gw'lanod i'w gweld yn fudr;
y blodau a'r perthi'n dal i sbecian,
ond fel pe bai eu tyfiant wedi ei atal
am ennyd fach,
er mwyn i rhywbeth arall llai llachar
gymeryd ei hynt.

Yfory, wedi'r dadmar,
fe ruthrwn ninnau'n ol i'r hen oruchwyliaeth.

SPRING SNOW

Today you fell, a silent white duvet,
on fields full of spring.
The roar of traffic was stilled,
and life slowed down as folk failed to reach work.
Your soft satire filled the air,
mocking those experts who thought
spring had come early.
You suggested the possibility of purity...
that this old world could be a better place,
with its people being more honest and clean;
not so much rushing and cursing,
money-grabbing and cheating.
This old earth had never been so white before
– whiter than white –
with the seagulls looking dirty;
shrubs and plants peeping out,
but as if slowing their growth
for a brief moment,
so that something else less showy
could take its course.

Tomorrow, after the thaw,
we'll all rush back to the old regime.

NEWID BYD

Mae'n fore yn yr harbwr a'r gwynt o'r mor yn ffein,
mae'r llongau wrth y lanfa, a'r trenau ar y lein;
mae'r hogia'n trin eu rhwydau, mae'n ferw yn yr iard,
mae'n brysur yn y stesion – dreifar, portar, giard.

Mae'n hwyrnos yn yr harbwr, daw'r gwynt o'r mor o hyd,
ond distaw ydyw'r gweithdai – daeth llawer tro ar fyd.
A ddaw y llongau eto i forio ar eu hynt?
A glywir hogia'n chwerthin fel yn y dyddiau gynt?

CHANGING TIMES

It's morning in the harbour, the sea breeze feels so fine,
with ships along the jetty, and trains upon the line;
the lads mend nets for fishing, there's bustle in the yards,
the station's full of people, with drivers, porters, guards.

It's midnight in the harbour, the sea-wind blowing cold,
but silent are the workers – not like the days of old.
Will ships once more come sailing, and drift towards the shore?
Will the lads again be laughing as in the days of yore?

LLEUAD FEDI

Lleuad Fedi, naw nos olau,
Tylwyth Teg ar hyd y cloddiau,
ninnau'n ifanc a dibryder
efo'n dyddiau i gyd o'n blaenau.

Lleuad Fedi uwch ein heinioes,
Hydref wedi cyrraedd eisoes;
dim ond Gaeaf sydd i ddilyn
a gweld colli ffrindiau cyfoes.

HARVEST MOON

Harvest Moon, nine nights of daylight,
Fairies dancing in our campsite,
and we, so young and full of fun,
with all our living to be done.

Harvest Moon, still there above us,
 Autumn's here and days are parlous,
Winter's coming, and not much fun
rememb'ring friends who have long gone

(A Harvest Moon apparently occurs in September or early October every 4 years or so, and it is a large and very bright moon which lasts for several nights. 'Lleuad Fedi' in Welsh means literally 'September Moon', and there was a belief in parts of rural Wales that it lasted nine nights, when it was light enough for farmers to bring in the harvest. It was also believed that, during this period, strange things were afoot...)

PRIODAS

Gwyn oedd lliw y diwrnod,
a gwyn oedd lliw ein byd,
a gwyn oedd lliw y geiriau
yngasom yno 'nghyd;
gwyn oedd lliw yr heulwen
a gwyn oedd lliw y coed,
a gwyn oedd pob adduned
wrth inni gadw'r oed.

Aeth deugain mlynedd heibio,
fe welsom lesni'r nef,
melynder haul yr hafddydd
a duwch storom gref;
profasom goch gwylltineb,
a gwyrdd eiddigedd ffol –
ond gwyn o hyd yw atgo
ein priodas 'mhell yn ol.

MARRIAGE

White was the day we wedded,
our world was coloured white,
and white the words we uttered
as one, to our delight;
and white describes the sunshine,
and white the trees above,
and white the vows we promised
pledging eternal love.

In forty years of marriage
we've lived 'neath azure sky,
the yellow sun of summer,
and black as storms came by;
were touched by red of anger,
the green of envy and more –
but white remains the mem'ry
of our marriage long ago.

LAPTOP

You sit on my lap,
waiting patiently,
blank white document ready,
cursor blinking,
waiting,
waiting,
waiting for me to create.

Do you remember, Timmy,
how you used to sit on my lap,
long ago?
Baby skin soft,
smelling of talc,
shaking with laughter
as I told you bedtime stories;
bouncing you up and down
and tickling your feet;
wishing you would stay like this for ever,
young and innocent...
just you and mammy and me?

Do you remember, Annie,
how you too used to sit on my lap,
long ago?
When we were young
and in love,
your skin soft to my touch,
the whiff of *chanel* behind your ear
lifting me high
into realms of romance?

And Timmy asleep in his cot,
and 'God in his heaven' as they say...

But since you've grown up, Timmy,
and left home...
and since you've died, Annie,
I can no longer create...

And the page on my laptop
remains blank...
the cursor still blinking,
waiting,
waiting...

COPING

'Isn't he coping well?'
'Marvellous!'
'And such a tragedy, wasn't it?'
I hear their voices, see their looks,
sympathetic, full of concern, kind.
'It happened so suddenly,' they say,
'and she wasn't even fifty!
And he's been so good, so brave,
so uncomplaining.'

I spend the days putting on a face,
- an actor applying his make-up -
putting on an act since she has gone;
stepping into costume,
walking on stage...
The show must go on.
Later, in the lonely safety of my home,
tears come.
Inside, I die again,
waiting for the final curtain
to fall.

SAPPHIRE DAY – SATURDAY 29 DECEMBER 2007
TO DIL 25.06.38 – 04.05.05

Today would have been our wedding anniversary;
forty-five years married –
our sapphire celebration.
That day too, long ago, like the stone
was blue and precious.
That day too, was a Saturday,
cold and icebound
in the winter
of `sixty-two.
But tho' we shivered
our love was warm,
and your eyes were blue, so very blue, and precious,
like the sapphire.
Today, I mourn your loss,
and wish those sapphire eyes
were looking into mine,
and your warm touch
thawing my heart.

NEW YEAR'S DAY CONCERT 2008
TO DIL 25.06.38 – 04.05.05

Do you remember
how we used to 'visit' Vienna
on New Year's Day?
How we 'attended'
the Golden Concert Hall of the Musikverein –
our television 'date' with the Philharmonic?
How we loved the Strauss waltzes
and the polkas?
How we entered the spirit
of the music and the place,
the beauty of the sound and scene,
and the light-footed dancers?
How we were carried high on wings of song
from our bleak Welsh winter
to romantic Austria?
How the uplifting music
gave us hope for another year?

Today, I watch alone
with memories of our love.
But I feel that you are very close to me,
this New Year's Day,
in romantic Vienna.

YELLOW ROSES
TO DIL 25.06.38 - 04.05.05
(on what would have been our Golden Wedding Anniversary 29.12.12)

Today, I buy yellow roses,
put them in a vase next to your photo;
dress decently but don't go out;
play music from *'West Side Story'* -
the very sound track of the film we shared
in London, on our honeymoon
fifty years ago.
Perhaps *somewhere* you still *feel pretty*,
and *tonight* I will love you again,
one hand, one heart.
All day long I paint precious pictures
in my mind -
half a century packed into fleeting hours.

Tomorrow, yellow roses
wither and die,
but memories remain
and love lives on
for ever...
and ever...
and ever...

I LOST YOU IN THE NIGHT
TO DIL 25.06.1938 – 04.05.2005

I lost you in the night,
in the dark,
in the still small hours,
before the first faint song of a hesitant bird
had broken the silence;
before the first glimmer
of a promised dawn;
before the moon had waned
and the stars had paled;
I lost you.

Your face was serene,
but your smile frozen,
and your body cold, so cold;
your eyes so still –
no time to say goodbye;
no time to say I loved you;
no time for plans unconsummated;
no time for dreams untold;
no time at all.

When morning came there was no dawn,
no light to permeate the dark,
no warmth to comfort me.
The silence screamed
as busy paramedics
took you away...
away from two score years and more
of being together;

away from the hopeful certainty of life,
of expected mornings
and days of sharing.

And I am cast adrift
on a sea of sadness and uncertainty...
Yet memories remain of sunny days,
of walking hand in hand in silence,
of vows and promises,
of births and hopes,
of what was and might have been,
of growing old together...

of the triumph of love.

Acknowledgements

The following poems were previously published in *'Spaces – 24th Anthology of The Chester* Poets' in August 2012:-
Childhood Home, Bulldozer, Cull of the Gods, Lost Love, Losers, Once Again, Soldiers, Miss Muffet and the Spider, Laptop, I Lost you in the Night.

I Lost you in the Night, previously titled *To My dear dead Wife,* was awarded First Prize in the Llandudno Area of the *Ottakar's and Faber Annual Poetry Competition* in 2006.

Twgi was previously published in *Cats, Cats, Cats – an Anthology of The Chester Poets* in 2013.

War Rations was previously published in *Through a Child's Eyes – Anthology of World War Two Poems, by Poetry Space Ltd,* in 2013.

Dawn was previously published in *Daily Reflections 2004, Triumph House, Peterborough.*

Escape into Celluloid was previously published in *Poetry Cornwall Issue 37,* as were the following bi-lingual poems:-
Newid Byd/Changing Times *(Issue 36),* **Priodas/Marriage** *(Issue 38),* **Lleuad Fedi/Harvest Moon** *(Issue 38),* all in 2013.

The following poems were previously published in *The Moving Finger – Magazine of Llandudno and District Writers*:-
Survival, previously titled *Silver Lining* in Summer 2012;
Right or Wrong? in Autumn 2012; **Scars of Battle** in Winter 2012-13; **Loneliness,** previously titled *I wandered lonely as a cloud* in Summer 2013.

Kingsmead is written in the style of a Welsh poem, *Cwm Alltcafan by T. Llew Jones.*